JOSEPH HAYDN

SYMPHONY No. 44

E minor/e-Moll/Mi mineur
Hob. I: 44
"Trauersinfonie"

Edited by/Herausgegeben von
H. C. Robbins Landon

Ernst Eulenburg Ltd

London · Mainz · Madrid · New York · Paris · Tokyo · Toronto · Zürich

Joseph Haydn,

Symphony No. 44 E minor (Trauer-Symphonie)

Haydn wrote this great and impassioned Symphony in E minor (No. 44) about 1771; no autograph survives, but the work was announced in the Breitkopf thematic catalogue of 1772 (Leipzig). The "Trauer" ("Mourning") Symphony, as it later came to be called, is by no means an isolated specimen, for between about 1768 and 1774 Haydn composed a number of works in the same intense style: *e.g.* the string Quartets of Opus 20 (1772); the opera *Philemon und Baucis* (1773); the *Stabat Mater* (*c*. 1767) and *Salve Regina* (1771), both in G minor; Symphonies 49 in F minor ("La Passione", 1768), 45 in F sharp minor ("Farewell", 1772), 52 in C minor (*c*. 1771-73); and the piano Sonata in C minor (No. 20, 1771). This sudden, glorious emergence of Haydn's maturity is thus chronicled in a series of works of various kinds.

The outer movements of the E minor Symphony show Haydn's newly found interest in motivic unity and in contrapuntal technique, while the sombre minuet, a strict "Canone in diapason", is a contrapuntal *tour-de-force* in itself. The *Adagio* and the trio, both in the tonic major, are among the most radiant and moving pieces in this whole remarkable period; one notices especially the novel use of the horn in both movements. But seldom has Haydn reached the emotional stress of the finale, particularly at the beginning of the development where, using a fragment of the first subject, the music rises to a pitch of almost unbearable intensity.

Incredible as it may seem, Haydn's Symphony No. 44 has never been printed in its authentic form. Even the earlier *Gesamtausgabe* (Serie I, Band 4, Leipzig, 1933, edited by Helmut Schultz) issued the work in the wrong sequence of movements, with many serious errors in dynamics, especially in the slow movements, with many serious errors in dynamics, especially in the slow movement, and even with a wrong note in the principal theme of the finale (bar 7, last note *e* instead of *f sharp*). The reader is referred to my book, *The Symphonies of Joseph Haydn*, London, 1955, pp. 682*ff.* for a list of sources and for the most important corrections to the text of the *Gesamtausgabe*.

The bassoon part is not specifically listed in any of the principal sources; but in Haydn's autographs of the period (*e.g.* Symphonies 43, 45, 47, 55) the bassoon frequently appears in the course of the work without being listed among the instruments required on the first page of the score. Moreover, in a letter of 1768, Haydn asks that the bassoon double the bass throughout a cantata, so that "certain passages . . . (may be) more clearly distinguished". For conductors wishing to use this edition, I have indicated my suggestion for the execution of the bassoon part in brackets, *i.e.* "con Fag." and "senza Fag."

Our new edition is based primarily on two of the earliest and most reliable manuscript sources, which are in orchestral parts:

(1) Fürstl. Thurn and Taxis Library, Regensburg, cat. J. Haydn 29. A very important manuscript of Viennese origin and the one which shows Haydn's intentions most clearly. In the early seventies, Regensburg seems to have received several shipments of Haydn symphonies (Nos. 42, 43, 44, 48, 54-57) from Vienna, possibly from the composer himself; the Thurn und Taxis copy of No. 48 ("Maria Theresia") is also the most reliable source extant, better even than the manuscript parts in the Esterházy Archives at Budapest. In Regensburg's copies of Nos. 44 and 48, we find the typical Haydn ornament

(a crossed turn: see No. 44, 1st movt., bars 19, 28 *ff.* and minuet, bars 12 *etc.*) which most copyists erroneously turned into trills. The execution of this ornament is similar to C.P.E. Bach's turn over a note, *i.e.* (No. 44, 1st. movement, bar 28, V. II).

(2) Monastery of Schlierbach, near Kremsmünster, Upper Austria. The watermarks of this source, which is also of Viennese origin, are in part the same as those of Joseph Elssler's copy of the Salve Regina (1771) in the Gesellschaft der Musikfreunde; although the watermarks are not certain evidence that the Schlierbach copy was made in 1771, other factors suggest that it is actually one of the earliest sources. In general, it is perhaps not so careful as the Regensburg copy; for instance, the above-mentioned ornaments are found as trills; but it was highly important for providing a check on certain details of the Regensburg copy which required confirmatory evidence.

Apart from these principal sources, the following additional manuscripts were used in determining the final text:

(3) Monastery of Melk, Lower Austria, cat. IV, 57.

(4) Monastery of Göttweig, Lower Austria, prepared by one of the local monks and signed "Comparavit P. Marianus [1]781".

(5) Monastery of Kremsmünster, Upper Austria, cat. H 5, 61. All three sources are of local origin and therefore at least one step away from the two principal manuscripts, textually speaking. Nevertheless, they often proved valuable in making decisions with regard to the placing of phrasing, dynamic marks, and the like. Apart from these five sources, which formed the textual basis of our edition, another twenty-one manuscripts and early printed editions were examined for the principal changes, such as the order of the movements. *None* of the early sources placed the minuet after the slow movement, and we may be assured that this was a typical nineteenth-century change, made at the earliest half-a-century after the symphony was written. The corrupted dynamic marks' in the *Gesamtausgabe's* text of the *Adagio* derive from one source only (a late copy in the Gesellschaft der Musikfreunde), as does the wrong note in bar 7 of the finale (see *supra*).

H. C. R. LANDON

Joseph Haydn, Symphonie GA 44, E-moll
("Trauer-Symphonie")

Diese bedeutende und leidenschaftliche Symphonie entstand um 1771; das Autograph ist nicht erhalten, aber das Werk wurde in dem thematischen Breitkopf-Katalog vom Jahre 1772 (Leipzig) angekündigt. Die "Trauer-Symphonie", wie sie später genannt wurde, trägt die charakteristischen Merkmale von Haydns Stil zwischen 1768 und 1774. Während dieses Zeitraums entstanden eine Reihe Werke ähnlicher innerer Spannung, wie die Quartette op. 20 (1772), die Oper "Philemon und Baucis" (1773), das "Stabat Mater" (ca. 1767) und das "Salve Regina" (1771), die beiden letzteren in G-moll, die Symphonien GA 49 in F-moll ("La Passione", 1768), GA 45 in Fis moll ("Abschiedssymphonie", 1772), GA 52 in C-moll (ca. 1771-73) und die Klavier-Sonate in C-moll (GA 20, 1771). Diese plötzlich beginnende Reife dokumentiert sich somit in Werken verschiedenster Art.

Die Ecksätze der E-moll-Symphonie zeigen Haydns neuerwachtes Interesse an motivischer Einheit und kontrapunktischem Satz, das düstere Menuett, ein streng durchgeführter "Canone in diapason", ist ein kontrapunktisches Bravourstück in sich selbst. Adagio und Trio, beide in der Dur-Variante, gehören zu den feinsten und innerlichsten Kompositionen dieser Periode; man bemerke besonders die neuartige Anwendung der Hörner. Im Finale aber gelingt Haydn eine selten vorher erreichte Stärke der gefühlsmässigen Intensität, besonders zu Beginn der Durchführung, wo sich durch Verarbeitung eines Fragments des ersten Themas ein Höhepunkt von grösster Spannung ergibt.

Von dieser Symphonie wurde niemals eine Neuausgabe in authentischer Form veröffentlicht. Selbst die Gesamtausgabe von Breitkopf & Härtel (Serie I, Bd. 4, Leipzig 1933, herausgegeben von Helmut Schultz) brachte das Werk in falscher Satzreihenfolge, mit zahlreichen schweren Fehlern der Dynamik (besonders im langsamen Satz) und sogar einer falschen Note im Hauptthema des Finale (T.7, letzte Note *e* statt *fis*). Hinsichtlich der Quellenliste und wichtigsten Korrekturen zum Text der Gesamtausgabe wird auf meine Publikation "The Symphonies of Joseph Haydn," London 1955, S.682ff., verwiesen.

Eine Fagottstimme ist in keiner der Hauptquellen gesondert notiert. In Haydns Autographen dieser Periode (wie die der Symphonien GA 43, 45, 47, 55) erscheint das Fagott oft im Verlauf des Werkes, ohne zu Beginn der Partitur angeführt zu werden. Weiters erklärt Haydn in einem Begleitbrief zu einer Kantate von 1768, dass das Fagott durchwegs den Bass verstärken solle, "weil sich gewisse Passagen hart distinguiren". Meine Vorschläge für die Ausführung der Fagottstimme sind in dieser Ausgabe durch Klammern erkenntlich ("con Fag." und "senza Fag.").

Unsere neue Ausgabe beruht hauptsächlich auf zwei der ältesten und zuverlässigsten MS.—Quellen in Stimmen:

(1) Fürstl. Thurn und Taxissche Bibliothek, Regensburg; Kat. J. Haydn 29. Ein sehr wichtiges MS. Wiener Herkunft, das Haydns Absichten am unverfälschtesten zu überliefern scheint. In den frühen 7oer Jahren dürfte Regensburg einige Sendungen von Haydn-Symphonien aus Wien, vielleicht vom Komponisten selbst, erhalten haben (GA 42, 43, 44, 48, 54-57); die dort befindliche Abschrift von GA 48 ("Maria Theresia") ist gleichfalls die zuverlässigste der uns überlieferten

Quellen, sie ist sogar genauer als die MS.-Stimmen des Esterházy-Archivs in Budapest. In den Regensburger Abschriften von GA 44 und 48 findet sich das typische Haydn-Ornament (ein durchstrichener Doppelschlag: vgl. GA 44, 1. Satz, T. 19, 28ff., sowie Menuett, T. 12 etc.), das von den meisten Kopisten fälschlich in einen Triller verwandelt wurde. Die Ausführung dieser Verzierung ist ähnlich der von Ph. E. Bachs Doppelschlag über der Note:

(GA. 44, 1. Satz, T. 28, VI. II).

(2) Stift Schlierbach (in der Nähe von Kremsmünster), Oberösterreich. Die Wasserzeichen dieser Quelle, ebenfalls Wiener Herkunft, sind zum Teil die gleichen wie die von Joseph Elsslers Abschrift des "Salve Regina" (1771) im Archiv der Gesellschaft der Musikfreunde, Wien. Daraus kann natürlich nicht der sichere Schluss gefasst werden, dass das Schlierbacher MS. gleichfalls aus dem Jahre 1771 stammt, doch führen andere Faktoren zu der Annahme, dass das MS. eine der ältesten Quellen ist. Allgemein gesehen zeigt es vielleicht nicht die Sorgfalt der Regensburger Stimmen (z.B. erscheinen die oben erwähnten Verzierungen als Triller), doch erwies sich das MS. zur Überprüfung gewisser Einzelheiten der Regensburger Stimmen, die der Bestätigung bedurften, als äusserst wichtig.

Ausser diesen zwei Hauptquellen wurden folgende MSS. zusätzlich zur Festlegung des endgültigen Textes herangezogen:

(3) Stift Melk, Niederösterreich, Kat. IV, 57.

(4) Stift Göttweig, Niederösterreich, von einem Stiftsangehörigen vorbereitet und signiert: "Comparavit P. Marianus [1]781."

(5) Stift Kremsmünster, Oberösterreich, Kat. H 5, 61.

Alle drei Quellen sind lokaler Herkunft, sie sind in textlicher Hinsicht mindestens einen Grad von den zwei Hauptquellen entfernt. Trotzdem erwies sich ihre Heranziehung in Phrasierungs- und Dynamikfragen als notwendig. Ausser diesen fünf Quellen, die die textliche Grundlage unserer Ausgabe bilden, wurden noch weitere 21 MSS. und frühe Drucke hinsichtlich der wichtigsten Änderungen, wie Reihenfolge der Sätze, geprüft. Keine der frühen Quellen stellt das Menuett hinter den langsamen Satz; sicher handelt es sich hier um einen typischen Eingriff des 19. Jahrhunderts, der frühestens ein halbes Jahrhundert nach der Entstehung der Symphonie erfolgte. Die korrumpierte Dynamik des Adagio im Text der Gesamtausgabe, sowie die falsche Note in T. 7 im Finale geht nur auf eine einzige Quelle (eine späte Abschrift in der Gesellschaft der Musikfreunde) zurück.

H. C. R. LANDON

Symphony No. 44
(Trauer)

I

Allegro con brio

Joseph Haydn
1732 — 1809

E.E.6091

Ernst Eulenburg Ltd

4

6

*) some sources

E.E. 6091

*) some sources

12

E.E. 6091

*) some sources

II

Menuetto

Allegretto

Canone in Diapason

Trio

Menuetto da capo

26

III

Adagio

Finale

IV

40

42